THE ULTIMATE STUDENT COMPANION

THIS PLANNER BELONGS TO

Name: _____

Address: _____

✉ _____

📞 _____

Copyright © 2021 Koschina L. Marshall

All rights reserved under the international copyright law. No part of this book may be reproduced or transmitted in any form or by any means, electronic or mechanical, including photocopying, recording, or by any information storage and retrieval system, without the express, written permission of the publisher or the author. The exception is reviewers, who may quote brief passages in a review.

Christian Living Books, Inc.
P. O. Box 7584
Largo, MD 20792 USA
christianlivingbooks.com
We bring your dreams to fruition.

ISBN 9781562295332

Conceive. Believe. Achieve. Succeed!

To the Source, Who is my provider, sustainer, peace, and the ultimate coach.

To my father, Charles "Chuck" Mackey, one of the most outstanding basketball coaches in the Commonwealth of The Bahamas. You coached many individuals in the game of basketball and life. You utilized your influence to secure university scholarships for the less fortunate. This assisted them in overcoming obstacles with the hope that they would maximize their potential. Now, the baton is in my hand to coach millions of students in the art of maximizing their potential in the classroom, university, and this game called life.

To all students, success comes from within. It is an insatiable desire to overcome obstacles and succeed. If you have this book in your hand, then you are already a success story. All you need now is the assistance of a Transformational Academic Coach to maximize the potential that is trapped within you.

ENDORSEMENTS

This student planner is a powerful learning tool! Get your copy today and rise to the highest level of learning because learning is an art, a joy, and a lifelong experience.

—Ralph Steele, Ph.D.
Oxford University, Oxford England,
Professor of Mediation & Structured Settlement Broker
Dallas, Texas, USA

Students at every level will benefit from using this student planner. Students need to organize their time well to learn as much as they can and achieve their educational goals. When students succeed in school, they are more likely to succeed in whatever they do after they graduate.

—John Lande, Ph.D.
Isidor Loeb Professor Emeritus
Senior Fellow, Center for the Study of Dispute Resolution
University of Missouri School of Law, USA

Our world needs an exceptional cadre of multitalented and multifaceted students who can chart the destiny of global civilization for the better. This student planner provides the perfect opportunity to guide your success by ensuring time management is instilled as a fundamental pillar of your work ethic environment.

—Hon. Saboto Caesar, LLB (Hons.) LLM, LEC
Minister of Agriculture, Forestry, Fisheries, Rural Transformation, Industry and Labour
St. Vincent and the Grenadines

Organization improves learning and increases the potential for success. Disorganization impedes learning and decreases the potential for success. In my 27 years of teaching, I can attest that those students who were organized, had a routine for managing time, and demonstrated good study habits had a better overall success rate in the classroom than their peers. This success was in direct relation to the use of a daily planner. A daily planner positively impacts learning. I highly recommend this diversified student planner.

—Trevor W. Wright, B.A., M.A.
Cert. Special Ed.
Loudoun County Public Schools, Virginia, USA

Brilliant and unique, this must-have student planner is highly recommended for high school students, especially seniors as they transition from high school into the real world. The guide is simple to use and promises to keep the user organized while enhancing time management skills. A must-have!

—**Carlene Davis-Williams, B.A., M.Ed.**
Veteran Educator 26 years, School Counselor
The Commonwealth of The Bahamas

Ms. Marshall has always emphasized the importance of planning and organization as essential tools for success. As her former student, I am honored to have been a beneficiary of her wealth of knowledge and skills in this area. Over the years, I have implemented many of her strategies during my studies, and much of my success can be attributed to the seeds she has planted. Today, as a dean and faculty member in higher education, I am now perfectly positioned to transfer these values for planning and organization to my students. I look forward to sharing this masterpiece with my students as a critical self-management tool for success.

—**Dr. Teo Cooper**
Dean/Assistant Professor of Science Education
University of The Bahamas

The best methodology to facilitate a more disciplined study pattern is to use a student planner! Koschina has designed this multifaceted student planner to assist students to effortlessly and strategically execute their study goals. I highly recommended it!

—**Lisa Wohlleb, BSc. Psychology**
Munich, Germany

There are many benefits of having a good student planner. As an educator of 24 years, I have seen how it gives students the freedom to keep track of their assignments and plan activities in an organized manner to create balance in their lives. A student planner of this caliber will definitely benefit students and aid them in managing their time effectively. I wish I had one during my time as a student!

—**Ismenette Victor, B.A., M.A.,**
Wilmington, Delaware, USA

The precision of Koschina's thoughts and artistry invested in designing this student planner is genuinely one of understanding the value of one's time in attaining one's educational endeavors. This student planner will help students remain intentional with the use of their time, achieve their goals steadily, and ultimately obtain successful results. I love this student planner because it is multifaceted! Get your copy today. I am confident your academic journey will be enhanced.

—**Jennifer Ducksworth, Ph.D.**
Former Academic Advisor
The University of Southern Mississippi and Georgia State University, USA

A student planner is an excellent tool that can assist any student in achieving top grades in school. This state-of-the-art student planner will help students stay organized with tests, projects, and even extracurricular activities. I encourage you to get your copy today and watch your child's academic success grow by leaps and bounds.

—**LaToya Greene, LLB (Hons.), LLM., LEC**
Nassau, The Bahamas

One of the biggest lessons I was taught in university is the importance of time management. Because I did not fully grasp the essence of this lifelong tool, sometimes I made costly missteps. In hindsight, I wish I had used a student planner during my high school and college tenure. It would have helped me to be more focused, organized, and deliberate as I navigated the demands of being a student. I wholeheartedly recommend this effective and versatile student planner.

—**Colbert Newry, BSc. (Dist.) Electrical Engineering**
Nassau, The Bahamas

When I became a college student for the first time, it would have been very beneficial to have an in-depth planner that Ms. Marshall designed! Besides studying, students usually take on extracurricular activities, so they need to understand how to manage their time adequately to accomplish their goals. Planners, like that of Ms. Marshall's, can assist students in being organized and aid in completing their activities effectively and efficiently.

—**Picandra K. Elzie, Doctoral Student**
Louisville, Kentucky, USA

As a former student of Ms. Marshall, I was taught the value of time management and organizational skills from junior high school to adulthood. These foundational skills helped to prepare me for national examinations, the rigors of university, and a professional designation. They also assisted in allowing me to have a strong work ethic. Ms. Marshall's sound advice and practices not only became core values, but a lifestyle. It continues to sustain my growth and development to this day, both professionally and personally.

—**Sanchina Rodgers, A.A. (Dist.), B.A, (Dist.) CPA**
Nassau, The Bahamas

CONTENTS

Introduction: The Ultimate Student Companion — 9

Part I: Start-Up Plan — 11
    1. Calendar References — 12
    2. Your Personalized Class Schedule — 13
    3. School Year Goals — 14
    4. Grade Tracker — 15

Part II: Focus and Organization Are Keys for Success — 19
Introduction to Part II — 20
    5. Weekly Planning Checklist — 22

Part III: Prioritize – Be Disciplined and Productive — 143
Introduction to Part III — 144
    6. Weekly Time Management Grid — 147

Part IV: I Made It! — 197
    7. Reflections on the Past School Year — 198
    8. Personal Reading List — 199
    9. Forecast for the Next School Year — 200

About the Author — 202
Bibliography — 203

CALENDAR REFERENCE

2025

January
Su	Mo	Tu	We	Th	Fr	Sa
			1	2	3	4
5	6	7	8	9	10	11
12	13	14	15	16	17	18
19	20	21	22	23	24	25
26	27	28	29	30	31	

February
Su	Mo	Tu	We	Th	Fr	Sa
						1
2	3	4	5	6	7	8
9	10	11	12	13	14	15
16	17	18	19	20	21	22
23	24	25	26	27	28	

March
Su	Mo	Tu	We	Th	Fr	Sa
						1
2	3	4	5	6	7	8
9	10	11	12	13	14	15
16	17	18	19	20	21	22
23	24	25	26	27	28	29
30	31					

April
Su	Mo	Tu	We	Th	Fr	Sa
		1	2	3	4	5
6	7	8	9	10	11	12
13	14	15	16	17	18	19
20	21	22	23	24	25	26
27	28	29	30			

May
Su	Mo	Tu	We	Th	Fr	Sa
				1	2	3
4	5	6	7	8	9	10
11	12	13	14	15	16	17
18	19	20	21	22	23	24
25	26	27	28	29	30	31

June
Su	Mo	Tu	We	Th	Fr	Sa
1	2	3	4	5	6	7
8	9	10	11	12	13	14
15	16	17	18	19	20	21
22	23	24	25	26	27	28
29	30					

July
Su	Mo	Tu	We	Th	Fr	Sa
		1	2	3	4	5
6	7	8	9	10	11	12
13	14	15	16	17	18	19
20	21	22	23	24	25	26
27	28	29	30	31		

August
Su	Mo	Tu	We	Th	Fr	Sa
					1	2
3	4	5	6	7	8	9
10	11	12	13	14	15	16
17	18	19	20	21	22	23
24	25	26	27	28	29	30
31						

September
Su	Mo	Tu	We	Th	Fr	Sa
	1	2	3	4	5	6
7	8	9	10	11	12	13
14	15	16	17	18	19	20
21	22	23	24	25	26	27
28	29	30				

October
Su	Mo	Tu	We	Th	Fr	Sa
			1	2	3	4
5	6	7	8	9	10	11
12	13	14	15	16	17	18
19	20	21	22	23	24	25
26	27	28	29	30	31	

November
Su	Mo	Tu	We	Th	Fr	Sa
						1
2	3	4	5	6	7	8
9	10	11	12	13	14	15
16	17	18	19	20	21	22
23	24	25	26	27	28	29
30						

December
Su	Mo	Tu	We	Th	Fr	Sa
	1	2	3	4	5	6
7	8	9	10	11	12	13
14	15	16	17	18	19	20
21	22	23	24	25	26	27
28	29	30	31			

2026

January
Su	Mo	Tu	We	Th	Fr	Sa
				1	2	3
4	5	6	7	8	9	10
11	12	13	14	15	16	17
18	19	20	21	22	23	24
25	26	27	28	29	30	31

February
Su	Mo	Tu	We	Th	Fr	Sa
1	2	3	4	5	6	7
8	9	10	11	12	13	14
15	16	17	18	19	20	21
22	23	24	25	26	27	28

March
Su	Mo	Tu	We	Th	Fr	Sa
1	2	3	4	5	6	7
8	9	10	11	12	13	14
15	16	17	18	19	20	21
22	23	24	25	26	27	28
29	30	31				

April
Su	Mo	Tu	We	Th	Fr	Sa
			1	2	3	4
5	6	7	8	9	10	11
12	13	14	15	16	17	18
19	20	21	22	23	24	25
26	27	28	29	30		

May
Su	Mo	Tu	We	Th	Fr	Sa
					1	2
3	4	5	6	7	8	9
10	11	12	13	14	15	16
17	18	19	20	21	22	23
24	25	26	27	28	29	30
31						

June
Su	Mo	Tu	We	Th	Fr	Sa
	1	2	3	4	5	6
7	8	9	10	11	12	13
14	15	16	17	18	19	20
21	22	23	24	25	26	27
28	29	30				

July
Su	Mo	Tu	We	Th	Fr	Sa
			1	2	3	4
5	6	7	8	9	10	11
12	13	14	15	16	17	18
19	20	21	22	23	24	25
26	27	28	29	30	31	

August
Su	Mo	Tu	We	Th	Fr	Sa
						1
2	3	4	5	6	7	8
9	10	11	12	13	14	15
16	17	18	19	20	21	22
23	24	25	26	27	28	29
30	31					

September
Su	Mo	Tu	We	Th	Fr	Sa
		1	2	3	4	5
6	7	8	9	10	11	12
13	14	15	16	17	18	19
20	21	22	23	24	25	26
27	28	29	30			

October
Su	Mo	Tu	We	Th	Fr	Sa
				1	2	3
4	5	6	7	8	9	10
11	12	13	14	15	16	17
18	19	20	21	22	23	24
25	26	27	28	29	30	31

November
Su	Mo	Tu	We	Th	Fr	Sa
1	2	3	4	5	6	7
8	9	10	11	12	13	14
15	16	17	18	19	20	21
22	23	24	25	26	27	**28**
29	30					

December
Su	Mo	Tu	We	Th	Fr	Sa
		1	2	3	4	5
6	7	8	9	10	11	12
13	14	15	16	17	18	19
20	21	22	23	24	25	26
27	28	29	30	31		

2027

January
Su	Mo	Tu	We	Th	Fr	Sa
					1	2
3	4	5	6	7	8	9
10	11	12	13	14	15	16
17	18	19	20	21	22	23
24	25	26	27	28	29	30
31						

February
Su	Mo	Tu	We	Th	Fr	Sa
	1	2	3	4	5	6
7	8	9	10	11	12	13
14	15	16	17	18	19	20
21	22	23	24	25	26	27
28						

March
Su	Mo	Tu	We	Th	Fr	Sa
	1	2	3	4	5	6
7	8	9	10	11	12	13
14	15	16	17	18	19	20
21	22	23	24	25	26	27
28	29	30	31			

April
Su	Mo	Tu	We	Th	Fr	Sa
				1	2	3
4	5	6	7	8	9	10
11	12	13	14	15	16	17
18	19	20	21	22	23	24
25	26	27	28	29	30	

May
Su	Mo	Tu	We	Th	Fr	Sa
						1
2	3	4	5	6	7	8
9	10	11	12	13	14	15
16	17	18	19	20	21	22
23	24	25	26	27	28	29
30	31					

June
Su	Mo	Tu	We	Th	Fr	Sa
		1	2	3	4	5
6	7	8	9	10	11	12
13	14	15	16	17	18	19
20	21	22	23	24	25	26
27	28	29	30			

July
Su	Mo	Tu	We	Th	Fr	Sa
				1	2	3
4	5	6	7	8	9	10
11	12	13	14	15	16	17
18	19	20	21	22	23	24
25	26	27	28	29	30	31

August
Su	Mo	Tu	We	Th	Fr	Sa
1	2	3	4	5	6	7
8	9	10	11	12	13	14
15	16	17	18	19	20	21
22	23	24	25	26	27	28
29	30	31				

September
Su	Mo	Tu	We	Th	Fr	Sa
			1	2	3	4
5	6	7	8	9	10	11
12	13	14	15	16	17	18
19	20	21	22	23	24	25
26	27	28	29	30		

October
Su	Mo	Tu	We	Th	Fr	Sa
					1	2
3	4	5	6	7	8	9
10	11	12	13	14	15	16
17	18	19	20	21	22	23
24	25	26	27	28	29	30
31						

November
Su	Mo	Tu	We	Th	Fr	Sa
	1	2	3	4	5	6
7	8	9	10	11	12	13
14	15	16	17	18	19	20
21	22	23	24	25	26	27
28	29	30				

December
Su	Mo	Tu	We	Th	Fr	Sa
			1	2	3	4
5	6	7	8	9	10	11
12	13	14	15	16	17	18
19	20	21	22	23	24	25
26	27	28	29	30	31	

INTRODUCTION

I will never forget a conversation I had with my uncle when I was thirteen years old. He began by asking me, "Are you an 'A' student or an 'F' student?" Then he went on to explain the difference between the two. He said, "the 'F' student is the person who lacks vision and never tries or aims to just get by. The 'A' student is the person who strives for the 'A' all the time. She may not get the 'A' every time, but true success will follow if she has an 'A' mentality." He said I should always strive to be the best at whatever I do.

Over the years, I have replayed these words of wisdom in my head and shared his counsel with my students. Now, I share it with you. Through my experience as a student and teacher, I discovered that a fundamental reason why students fail to maximize their full potential is due to their lack of focus, organization, and discipline. To fill this void, I have taken my years of experience as a student and teacher and designed a one-of-a-kind student planner, which is the ultimate student companion. Its goal is to help students become focused, organized, and disciplined.

Every feature in this student planner was designed with the student in mind. You can use it as a workbook in middle school, high school, college, or university. Learn a new word every week. Embrace weekly affirmations. Track your grades regularly. Be motivated by famous quotes by successful people. Keep all your school administrative materials in one place, for example, your class schedule and essential school dates. Decide on your overall goals for each week and the entire school year.

Record all your homework assignments, extracurricular activities, deadlines for pending assignments, other academic tasks, exam and quiz dates in the Weekly Planning Checklist. Manage your time wisely by consistently and adequately using the Weekly Time Management Grid to stay focused and organized, practice self-discipline, and be productive this school year.

This student planner is for every student – procrastinator or overachiever – especially if you lack organization skills, easily lose focus, or get overwhelmed with the day-to-day hustle of being a student. If you commit to using this student planner and execute the instructions provided within, I am confident you will see an improvement in your grades.

Students, I encourage you to rise to the occasion and maximize the potential trapped within you. Stay focused, organized, and determined. Remember, if you can conceive and believe it, you will achieve whatever you put your mind to do. You *will* be successful! Why not do the work to obtain success in whatever you do? Commit to using this student planner. Give it your all!

★ Part I ★

Start-Up PLAN

CLASS Schedule

⏰	MONDAY	TUESDAY	WEDNESDAY	THURSDAY	FRIDAY
8 – 9					
9 – 10					
10 – 11					
11 – 12					
12 – 1					
1 – 2					
2 – 3					
3 – 4					
4 – 5					
5 – 6					
6 – 7					
7 – 8					
8 – 9					

Notes _____

_____

_____

PART I: START-UP PLAN

	SCHOOL YEAR GOALS	Completed
1		☆
2		☆
3		☆
4		☆
5		☆
6		☆
7		☆
8		☆
9		☆
10		☆
11		☆
12		☆
13		☆
14		☆
15		☆
16		☆
17		☆

GRADE *Tracker*

Subject:

NO	DATE	ASSIGNMENT/QUIZ/EXAM	GRADE

Subject:

NO.	DATE	ASSIGNMENT/QUIZ/EXAM	GRADE

GRADE

Subject:

NO	DATE	ASSIGNMENT/QUIZ/EXAM	GRADE

Subject:

NO	DATE	ASSIGNMENT/QUIZ/EXAM	GRADE

GRADE *Tracker*

Subject:

NO	DATE	ASSIGNMENT/QUIZ/EXAM	GRADE

Subject:

NO	DATE	ASSIGNMENT/QUIZ/EXAM	GRADE

GRADE Tracker

Subject:

NO	DATE	ASSIGNMENT/QUIZ/EXAM	GRADE

Subject:

NO	DATE	ASSIGNMENT/QUIZ/EXAM	GRADE

★ Part II ★

Focus AND Organization
ARE KEYS FOR SUCCESS

INTRODUCTION TO PART II

To be successful, you need to work hard, but you must also learn to work smart. One way to do this is to be focused and organized. Just think, what would happen if you had multiple homework assignments, tests in multiple subjects, and a project, all due the same week, but you failed to be focused and organized? Benjamin Franklin famously said, "If you fail to plan, you are planning to fail." A lack of focus and organization can wreak havoc in your life and lead to avoidable failure.

WHAT IS THE WEEKLY PLANNING CHECKLIST?

The goal of the Weekly Planning Checklist is to assist students in becoming focused and organized.

Students should record all homework assignments, extracurricular activities, deadlines for pending assignments, exam/quiz dates, and other academic tasks in the Weekly Planning Checklist. Be sure to account for all academic tasks.

Update the Weekly Planning Checklist daily, and plan for each coming week throughout the school year. Take your time to carefully fill out this section. The Weekly Planning Checklist will also help to guide your Weekly Time Management Grid.

"FOCUS" AND "ORGANIZATION" ARE YOUR BUZZWORDS

The more you commit to using the Weekly Planning Checklist, the more focused and organized it will help you become. At first, it may seem as if significant extra time and energy are being channeled into this section, and you may get tired and frustrated. However, as with any new habit, if you sick with it, you will get better at it. This checklist will help you succeed, reduce stress, decrease chaos in your life, and become more disciplined.

EVALUATION

Remember to place a check mark in the Done column to signify when you have finished a task. At the end of each week, evaluate your progress and reschedule any tasks you did not complete.

WORD OF THE WEEK

I encourage you to search the dictionary for a new word every week. Write the word and its definition in the section provided, and practice using the word for one week. Eventually, if you commit to using the new word, it will become a normal part of your vocabulary.

SET GOALS

Make sure to set achievable goals each week and evaluate whether you have accomplished them at the end of each week. If you fail to accomplish your weekly goals, try to achieve them the following week.

MONTH:

NOTES	SUNDAY	MONDAY	TUESDAY

WEDNESDAY	THURSDAY	FRIDAY	SATURDAY
☐	☐	☐	☐
☐	☐	☐	☐
☐	☐	☐	☐
☐	☐	☐	☐
☐	☐	☐	☐

WEEKLY PLANNING CHECKLIST — WEEK OF

This week's goals are: ....
....

MONDAY	Due Date	Done
		☐
		☐
		☐
		☐
		☐
		☐

TUESDAY	Due Date	Done
		☐
		☐
		☐
		☐
		☐
		☐

WEDNESDAY	Due Date	Done
		☐
		☐
		☐
		☐
		☐
		☐

📖 **WORD OF THE WEEK**

THURSDAY	Due Date	Done
		☐
		☐
		☐
		☐
		☐
		☐

FRIDAY	Due Date	Done
		☐
		☐
		☐
		☐
		☐
		☐

SATURDAY	Due Date	Done
		☐
		☐
		☐
		☐
		☐
		☐

SUNDAY	Due Date	Done
		☐
		☐
		☐
		☐
		☐
		☐

WEEKLY PLANNING CHECKLIST — WEEK OF

This week's goals are: ....
....

MONDAY	Due Date	Done
		☐
		☐
		☐
		☐
		☐
		☐

TUESDAY	Due Date	Done
		☐
		☐
		☐
		☐
		☐
		☐

WEDNESDAY	Due Date	Done
		☐
		☐
		☐
		☐
		☐
		☐

📖 **WORD OF THE WEEK**

THURSDAY	Due Date	Done
		☐
		☐
		☐
		☐
		☐
		☐

FRIDAY	Due Date	Done
		☐
		☐
		☐
		☐
		☐
		☐

SATURDAY	Due Date	Done
		☐
		☐
		☐
		☐
		☐
		☐

SUNDAY	Due Date	Done
		☐
		☐
		☐
		☐
		☐
		☐

WEEKLY PLANNING CHECKLIST `WEEK OF`

This week's goals are: ....
....

MONDAY	Due Date	Done
		☐
		☐
		☐
		☐
		☐
		☐

TUESDAY	Due Date	Done
		☐
		☐
		☐
		☐
		☐
		☐

WEDNESDAY	Due Date	Done
		☐
		☐
		☐
		☐
		☐
		☐

📖 **WORD OF THE WEEK**

THURSDAY	Due Date	Done
		☐
		☐
		☐
		☐
		☐
		☐

FRIDAY	Due Date	Done
		☐
		☐
		☐
		☐
		☐
		☐

SATURDAY	Due Date	Done
		☐
		☐
		☐
		☐
		☐
		☐

SUNDAY	Due Date	Done
		☐
		☐
		☐
		☐
		☐
		☐

WEEKLY PLANNING CHECKLIST — WEEK OF

This week's goals are: ....
....

MONDAY	Due Date	Done
		☐
		☐
		☐
		☐
		☐
		☐

TUESDAY	Due Date	Done
		☐
		☐
		☐
		☐
		☐
		☐

WEDNESDAY	Due Date	Done
		☐
		☐
		☐
		☐
		☐
		☐

📖 **WORD OF THE WEEK**

PART II: FOCUS AND ORGANIZATION ARE KEYS FOR SUCCESS

THURSDAY	Due Date	Done
		☐
		☐
		☐
		☐
		☐
		☐

FRIDAY	Due Date	Done
		☐
		☐
		☐
		☐
		☐
		☐

SATURDAY	Due Date	Done
		☐
		☐
		☐
		☐
		☐
		☐

SUNDAY	Due Date	Done
		☐
		☐
		☐
		☐
		☐
		☐

WEEKLY PLANNING CHECKLIST WEEK OF

This week's goals are: ....
....

MONDAY	Due Date	Done
		☐
		☐
		☐
		☐
		☐
		☐

TUESDAY	Due Date	Done
		☐
		☐
		☐
		☐
		☐
		☐

WEDNESDAY	Due Date	Done
		☐
		☐
		☐
		☐
		☐
		☐

📖 **WORD OF THE WEEK**

PART II: FOCUS AND ORGANIZATION ARE KEYS FOR SUCCESS 33

THURSDAY	Due Date	Done
		☐
		☐
		☐
		☐
		☐
		☐

FRIDAY	Due Date	Done
		☐
		☐
		☐
		☐
		☐
		☐

SATURDAY	Due Date	Done
		☐
		☐
		☐
		☐
		☐
		☐

SUNDAY	Due Date	Done
		☐
		☐
		☐
		☐
		☐
		☐

MONTH:

NOTES	SUNDAY	MONDAY	TUESDAY
	☐	☐	☐
	☐	☐	☐
	☐	☐	☐
	☐	☐	☐
	☐	☐	☐

WEDNESDAY	THURSDAY	FRIDAY	SATURDAY

WEEKLY PLANNING CHECKLIST   WEEK OF

This week's goals are: ....
....

MONDAY	Due Date	Done
		☐
		☐
		☐
		☐
		☐
		☐

TUESDAY	Due Date	Done
		☐
		☐
		☐
		☐
		☐
		☐

WEDNESDAY	Due Date	Done
		☐
		☐
		☐
		☐
		☐
		☐

📖 WORD OF THE WEEK

THURSDAY	Due Date	Done
		☐
		☐
		☐
		☐
		☐
		☐

FRIDAY	Due Date	Done
		☐
		☐
		☐
		☐
		☐
		☐

SATURDAY	Due Date	Done
		☐
		☐
		☐
		☐
		☐
		☐

SUNDAY	Due Date	Done
		☐
		☐
		☐
		☐
		☐
		☐

WEEKLY PLANNING CHECKLIST   WEEK OF

This week's goals are: ....
....

MONDAY	Due Date	Done
		☐
		☐
		☐
		☐
		☐
		☐

TUESDAY	Due Date	Done
		☐
		☐
		☐
		☐
		☐
		☐

WEDNESDAY	Due Date	Done
		☐
		☐
		☐
		☐
		☐
		☐

WORD OF THE WEEK

THURSDAY	Due Date	Done
		☐
		☐
		☐
		☐
		☐
		☐

FRIDAY	Due Date	Done
		☐
		☐
		☐
		☐
		☐
		☐

SATURDAY	Due Date	Done
		☐
		☐
		☐
		☐
		☐
		☐

SUNDAY	Due Date	Done
		☐
		☐
		☐
		☐
		☐
		☐

WEEKLY PLANNING CHECKLIST WEEK OF

This week's goals are: ....
....

MONDAY	Due Date	Done
		☐
		☐
		☐
		☐
		☐
		☐

TUESDAY	Due Date	Done
		☐
		☐
		☐
		☐
		☐
		☐

WEDNESDAY	Due Date	Done
		☐
		☐
		☐
		☐
		☐
		☐

📖 **WORD OF THE WEEK**

THURSDAY	Due Date	Done
		☐
		☐
		☐
		☐
		☐
		☐

FRIDAY	Due Date	Done
		☐
		☐
		☐
		☐
		☐
		☐

SATURDAY	Due Date	Done
		☐
		☐
		☐
		☐
		☐
		☐

SUNDAY	Due Date	Done
		☐
		☐
		☐
		☐
		☐
		☐

WEEKLY PLANNING CHECKLIST **WEEK OF**

This week's goals are: ....
....

MONDAY	Due Date	Done
		☐
		☐
		☐
		☐
		☐
		☐

TUESDAY	Due Date	Done
		☐
		☐
		☐
		☐
		☐
		☐

WEDNESDAY	Due Date	Done
		☐
		☐
		☐
		☐
		☐
		☐

📖 **WORD OF THE WEEK**

THURSDAY	Due Date	Done
		☐
		☐
		☐
		☐
		☐
		☐

FRIDAY	Due Date	Done
		☐
		☐
		☐
		☐
		☐
		☐

SATURDAY	Due Date	Done
		☐
		☐
		☐
		☐
		☐
		☐

SUNDAY	Due Date	Done
		☐
		☐
		☐
		☐
		☐
		☐

WEEKLY PLANNING CHECKLIST WEEK OF

This week's goals are: ....
....

MONDAY	Due Date	Done
		☐
		☐
		☐
		☐
		☐
		☐

TUESDAY	Due Date	Done
		☐
		☐
		☐
		☐
		☐
		☐

WEDNESDAY	Due Date	Done
		☐
		☐
		☐
		☐
		☐
		☐

📖 **WORD OF THE WEEK**

THURSDAY	Due Date	Done
		☐
		☐
		☐
		☐
		☐
		☐

FRIDAY	Due Date	Done
		☐
		☐
		☐
		☐
		☐
		☐

SATURDAY	Due Date	Done
		☐
		☐
		☐
		☐
		☐
		☐

SUNDAY	Due Date	Done
		☐
		☐
		☐
		☐
		☐
		☐

MONTH:

NOTES	SUNDAY	MONDAY	TUESDAY
	☐	☐	☐
	☐	☐	☐
	☐	☐	☐
	☐	☐	☐
	☐	☐	☐

PART II: FOCUS AND ORGANIZATION ARE KEYS FOR SUCCESS

WEDNESDAY	THURSDAY	FRIDAY	SATURDAY

WEEKLY PLANNING CHECKLIST **WEEK OF**

This week's goals are: ....
....

MONDAY	Due Date	Done
		☐
		☐
		☐
		☐
		☐
		☐

TUESDAY	Due Date	Done
		☐
		☐
		☐
		☐
		☐
		☐

WEDNESDAY	Due Date	Done
		☐
		☐
		☐
		☐
		☐
		☐

📖 **WORD OF THE WEEK**

THURSDAY	Due Date	Done
		☐
		☐
		☐
		☐
		☐
		☐

FRIDAY	Due Date	Done
		☐
		☐
		☐
		☐
		☐
		☐

SATURDAY	Due Date	Done
		☐
		☐
		☐
		☐
		☐
		☐

SUNDAY	Due Date	Done
		☐
		☐
		☐
		☐
		☐
		☐

WEEKLY PLANNING CHECKLIST — WEEK OF

This week's goals are:

MONDAY	Due Date	Done
		☐
		☐
		☐
		☐
		☐
		☐

TUESDAY	Due Date	Done
		☐
		☐
		☐
		☐
		☐
		☐

WEDNESDAY	Due Date	Done
		☐
		☐
		☐
		☐
		☐
		☐

WORD OF THE WEEK

THURSDAY | Due Date | Done

FRIDAY | Due Date | Done

SATURDAY | Due Date | Done

SUNDAY | Due Date | Done

WEEKLY PLANNING CHECKLIST **WEEK OF**

This week's goals are:

MONDAY	Due Date	Done
		☐
		☐
		☐
		☐
		☐
		☐

TUESDAY	Due Date	Done
		☐
		☐
		☐
		☐
		☐
		☐

WEDNESDAY	Due Date	Done
		☐
		☐
		☐
		☐
		☐
		☐

📖 **WORD OF THE WEEK**

THURSDAY	Due Date	Done
		☐
		☐
		☐
		☐
		☐
		☐

FRIDAY	Due Date	Done
		☐
		☐
		☐
		☐
		☐
		☐

SATURDAY	Due Date	Done
		☐
		☐
		☐
		☐
		☐
		☐

SUNDAY	Due Date	Done
		☐
		☐
		☐
		☐
		☐
		☐

WEEKLY PLANNING CHECKLIST WEEK OF

This week's goals are:

MONDAY	Due Date	Done
		☐
		☐
		☐
		☐
		☐
		☐

TUESDAY	Due Date	Done
		☐
		☐
		☐
		☐
		☐
		☐

WEDNESDAY	Due Date	Done
		☐
		☐
		☐
		☐
		☐
		☐

📖 **WORD OF THE WEEK**

THURSDAY	Due Date	Done
		☐
		☐
		☐
		☐
		☐
		☐

FRIDAY	Due Date	Done
		☐
		☐
		☐
		☐
		☐
		☐

SATURDAY	Due Date	Done
		☐
		☐
		☐
		☐
		☐
		☐

SUNDAY	Due Date	Done
		☐
		☐
		☐
		☐
		☐
		☐

WEEKLY PLANNING CHECKLIST — WEEK OF

This week's goals are: ....
....

MONDAY	Due Date	Done
		☐
		☐
		☐
		☐
		☐
		☐

TUESDAY	Due Date	Done
		☐
		☐
		☐
		☐
		☐
		☐

WEDNESDAY	Due Date	Done
		☐
		☐
		☐
		☐
		☐
		☐

📖 **WORD OF THE WEEK**

PART II: FOCUS AND ORGANIZATION ARE KEYS FOR SUCCESS

THURSDAY	Due Date	Done
		☐
		☐
		☐
		☐
		☐
		☐

FRIDAY	Due Date	Done
		☐
		☐
		☐
		☐
		☐
		☐

SATURDAY	Due Date	Done
		☐
		☐
		☐
		☐
		☐
		☐

SUNDAY	Due Date	Done
		☐
		☐
		☐
		☐
		☐
		☐

MONTH:

NOTES	SUNDAY	MONDAY	TUESDAY
	☐	☐	☐
	☐	☐	☐
	☐	☐	☐
	☐	☐	☐
	☐	☐	☐

WEDNESDAY	THURSDAY	FRIDAY	SATURDAY

WEEKLY PLANNING CHECKLIST `WEEK OF`

This week's goals are: ....
....

MONDAY	Due Date	Done
		☐
		☐
		☐
		☐
		☐
		☐

TUESDAY	Due Date	Done
		☐
		☐
		☐
		☐
		☐
		☐

WEDNESDAY	Due Date	Done
		☐
		☐
		☐
		☐
		☐
		☐

📕 WORD OF THE WEEK

THURSDAY	Due Date	Done
		☐
		☐
		☐
		☐
		☐
		☐

FRIDAY	Due Date	Done
		☐
		☐
		☐
		☐
		☐
		☐

SATURDAY	Due Date	Done
		☐
		☐
		☐
		☐
		☐
		☐

SUNDAY	Due Date	Done
		☐
		☐
		☐
		☐
		☐
		☐

WEEKLY PLANNING CHECKLIST   WEEK OF

This week's goals are:

MONDAY	Due Date	Done
		☐
		☐
		☐
		☐
		☐
		☐

TUESDAY	Due Date	Done
		☐
		☐
		☐
		☐
		☐
		☐

WEDNESDAY	Due Date	Done
		☐
		☐
		☐
		☐
		☐
		☐

📖 **WORD OF THE WEEK**

THURSDAY	Due Date	Done
		☐
		☐
		☐
		☐
		☐
		☐

FRIDAY	Due Date	Done
		☐
		☐
		☐
		☐
		☐
		☐

SATURDAY	Due Date	Done
		☐
		☐
		☐
		☐
		☐
		☐

SUNDAY	Due Date	Done
		☐
		☐
		☐
		☐
		☐
		☐

WEEKLY PLANNING CHECKLIST `WEEK OF`

This week's goals are: ....
....

MONDAY	Due Date	Done
		☐
		☐
		☐
		☐
		☐
		☐

TUESDAY	Due Date	Done
		☐
		☐
		☐
		☐
		☐
		☐

WEDNESDAY	Due Date	Done
		☐
		☐
		☐
		☐
		☐
		☐

📕 **WORD OF THE WEEK**

PART II: FOCUS AND ORGANIZATION ARE KEYS FOR SUCCESS

THURSDAY	Due Date	Done
		☐
		☐
		☐
		☐
		☐
		☐

FRIDAY	Due Date	Done
		☐
		☐
		☐
		☐
		☐
		☐

SATURDAY	Due Date	Done
		☐
		☐
		☐
		☐
		☐
		☐

SUNDAY	Due Date	Done
		☐
		☐
		☐
		☐
		☐
		☐

WEEKLY PLANNING CHECKLIST `WEEK OF`

This week's goals are:

MONDAY	Due Date	Done
		☐
		☐
		☐
		☐
		☐
		☐

TUESDAY	Due Date	Done
		☐
		☐
		☐
		☐
		☐
		☐

WEDNESDAY	Due Date	Done
		☐
		☐
		☐
		☐
		☐
		☐

📖 **WORD OF THE WEEK**

THURSDAY	Due Date	Done
		☐
		☐
		☐
		☐
		☐
		☐

FRIDAY	Due Date	Done
		☐
		☐
		☐
		☐
		☐
		☐

SATURDAY	Due Date	Done
		☐
		☐
		☐
		☐
		☐
		☐

SUNDAY	Due Date	Done
		☐
		☐
		☐
		☐
		☐
		☐

WEEKLY PLANNING CHECKLIST **WEEK OF**

This week's goals are: ....
....

MONDAY	Due Date	Done
		☐
		☐
		☐
		☐
		☐
		☐

TUESDAY	Due Date	Done
		☐
		☐
		☐
		☐
		☐
		☐

WEDNESDAY	Due Date	Done
		☐
		☐
		☐
		☐
		☐
		☐

📕 **WORD OF THE WEEK**

THURSDAY	Due Date	Done
		☐
		☐
		☐
		☐
		☐
		☐

FRIDAY	Due Date	Done
		☐
		☐
		☐
		☐
		☐
		☐

SATURDAY	Due Date	Done
		☐
		☐
		☐
		☐
		☐
		☐

SUNDAY	Due Date	Done
		☐
		☐
		☐
		☐
		☐
		☐

MONTH:

NOTES	SUNDAY	MONDAY	TUESDAY
	☐	☐	☐
	☐	☐	☐
	☐	☐	☐
	☐	☐	☐
	☐	☐	☐

WEDNESDAY	THURSDAY	FRIDAY	SATURDAY

WEEKLY PLANNING CHECKLIST `WEEK OF`

This week's goals are: ....
....

MONDAY	Due Date	Done
		☐
		☐
		☐
		☐
		☐
		☐

TUESDAY	Due Date	Done
		☐
		☐
		☐
		☐
		☐
		☐

WEDNESDAY	Due Date	Done
		☐
		☐
		☐
		☐
		☐
		☐

📖 **WORD OF THE WEEK**

THURSDAY	Due Date	Done
		☐
		☐
		☐
		☐
		☐
		☐

FRIDAY	Due Date	Done
		☐
		☐
		☐
		☐
		☐
		☐

SATURDAY	Due Date	Done
		☐
		☐
		☐
		☐
		☐
		☐

SUNDAY	Due Date	Done
		☐
		☐
		☐
		☐
		☐
		☐

WEEKLY PLANNING CHECKLIST — WEEK OF

This week's goals are: ....
....

MONDAY	Due Date	Done
		☐
		☐
		☐
		☐
		☐
		☐

TUESDAY	Due Date	Done
		☐
		☐
		☐
		☐
		☐
		☐

WEDNESDAY	Due Date	Done
		☐
		☐
		☐
		☐
		☐
		☐

📕 **WORD OF THE WEEK**

THURSDAY	Due Date	Done
		☐
		☐
		☐
		☐
		☐
		☐

FRIDAY	Due Date	Done
		☐
		☐
		☐
		☐
		☐
		☐

SATURDAY	Due Date	Done
		☐
		☐
		☐
		☐
		☐
		☐

SUNDAY	Due Date	Done
		☐
		☐
		☐
		☐
		☐
		☐

WEEKLY PLANNING CHECKLIST   WEEK OF

This week's goals are:

MONDAY	Due Date	Done
		☐
		☐
		☐
		☐
		☐
		☐

TUESDAY	Due Date	Done
		☐
		☐
		☐
		☐
		☐
		☐

WEDNESDAY	Due Date	Done
		☐
		☐
		☐
		☐
		☐
		☐

📖 **WORD OF THE WEEK**

THURSDAY	**Due Date**	**Done**
		☐
		☐
		☐
		☐
		☐
		☐

FRIDAY	**Due Date**	**Done**
		☐
		☐
		☐
		☐
		☐
		☐

SATURDAY	**Due Date**	**Done**
		☐
		☐
		☐
		☐
		☐
		☐

SUNDAY	**Due Date**	**Done**
		☐
		☐
		☐
		☐
		☐
		☐

WEEKLY PLANNING CHECKLIST — WEEK OF

This week's goals are: ....
....

MONDAY	Due Date	Done
		☐
		☐
		☐
		☐
		☐
		☐

TUESDAY	Due Date	Done
		☐
		☐
		☐
		☐
		☐
		☐

WEDNESDAY	Due Date	Done
		☐
		☐
		☐
		☐
		☐
		☐

📖 WORD OF THE WEEK

THURSDAY	Due Date	Done
		☐
		☐
		☐
		☐
		☐
		☐

FRIDAY	Due Date	Done
		☐
		☐
		☐
		☐
		☐
		☐

SATURDAY	Due Date	Done
		☐
		☐
		☐
		☐
		☐
		☐

SUNDAY	Due Date	Done
		☐
		☐
		☐
		☐
		☐
		☐

WEEKLY PLANNING CHECKLIST   `WEEK OF`

This week's goals are: ....
....

MONDAY	Due Date	Done
		☐
		☐
		☐
		☐
		☐
		☐

TUESDAY	Due Date	Done
		☐
		☐
		☐
		☐
		☐
		☐

WEDNESDAY	Due Date	Done
		☐
		☐
		☐
		☐
		☐
		☐

📕 **WORD OF THE WEEK**

THURSDAY	Due Date	Done
		☐
		☐
		☐
		☐
		☐
		☐

FRIDAY	Due Date	Done
		☐
		☐
		☐
		☐
		☐
		☐

SATURDAY	Due Date	Done
		☐
		☐
		☐
		☐
		☐
		☐

SUNDAY	Due Date	Done
		☐
		☐
		☐
		☐
		☐
		☐

MONTH:

NOTES	SUNDAY	MONDAY	TUESDAY
	☐	☐	☐
	☐	☐	☐
	☐	☐	☐
	☐	☐	☐
	☐	☐	☐

WEDNESDAY	THURSDAY	FRIDAY	SATURDAY
☐	☐	☐	☐
☐	☐	☐	☐
☐	☐	☐	☐
☐	☐	☐	☐
☐	☐	☐	☐

WEEKLY PLANNING CHECKLIST `WEEK OF`

This week's goals are: ....
....

MONDAY	Due Date	Done
		☐
		☐
		☐
		☐
		☐
		☐

TUESDAY	Due Date	Done
		☐
		☐
		☐
		☐
		☐
		☐

WEDNESDAY	Due Date	Done
		☐
		☐
		☐
		☐
		☐
		☐

📓 **WORD OF THE WEEK**

THURSDAY | | Due Date | Done

	Due Date	Done
		☐
		☐
		☐
		☐
		☐
		☐

FRIDAY

	Due Date	Done
		☐
		☐
		☐
		☐
		☐
		☐

SATURDAY

	Due Date	Done
		☐
		☐
		☐
		☐
		☐
		☐

SUNDAY

	Due Date	Done
		☐
		☐
		☐
		☐
		☐
		☐

WEEKLY PLANNING CHECKLIST   WEEK OF

This week's goals are: ....
....

MONDAY	Due Date	Done
		☐
		☐
		☐
		☐
		☐
		☐

TUESDAY	Due Date	Done
		☐
		☐
		☐
		☐
		☐
		☐

WEDNESDAY	Due Date	Done
		☐
		☐
		☐
		☐
		☐
		☐

📙 **WORD OF THE WEEK**

THURSDAY	Due Date	Done
		☐
		☐
		☐
		☐
		☐
		☐

FRIDAY	Due Date	Done
		☐
		☐
		☐
		☐
		☐
		☐

SATURDAY	Due Date	Done
		☐
		☐
		☐
		☐
		☐
		☐

SUNDAY	Due Date	Done
		☐
		☐
		☐
		☐
		☐
		☐

WEEKLY PLANNING CHECKLIST   WEEK OF

This week's goals are: ....
....

MONDAY	Due Date	Done
		☐
		☐
		☐
		☐
		☐
		☐

TUESDAY	Due Date	Done
		☐
		☐
		☐
		☐
		☐
		☐

WEDNESDAY	Due Date	Done
		☐
		☐
		☐
		☐
		☐
		☐

📖 **WORD OF THE WEEK**

THURSDAY	Due Date	Done
		☐
		☐
		☐
		☐
		☐
		☐

FRIDAY	Due Date	Done
		☐
		☐
		☐
		☐
		☐
		☐

SATURDAY	Due Date	Done
		☐
		☐
		☐
		☐
		☐
		☐

SUNDAY	Due Date	Done
		☐
		☐
		☐
		☐
		☐
		☐

WEEKLY PLANNING CHECKLIST **WEEK OF**

This week's goals are: ....
....

MONDAY	Due Date	Done
		☐
		☐
		☐
		☐
		☐
		☐

TUESDAY	Due Date	Done
		☐
		☐
		☐
		☐
		☐
		☐

WEDNESDAY	Due Date	Done
		☐
		☐
		☐
		☐
		☐
		☐

📖 **WORD OF THE WEEK**

THURSDAY	Due Date	Done
		☐
		☐
		☐
		☐
		☐
		☐

FRIDAY	Due Date	Done
		☐
		☐
		☐
		☐
		☐
		☐

SATURDAY	Due Date	Done
		☐
		☐
		☐
		☐
		☐
		☐

SUNDAY	Due Date	Done
		☐
		☐
		☐
		☐
		☐
		☐

WEEKLY PLANNING CHECKLIST WEEK OF

This week's goals are: ....
....

MONDAY	Due Date	Done
		☐
		☐
		☐
		☐
		☐
		☐

TUESDAY	Due Date	Done
		☐
		☐
		☐
		☐
		☐
		☐

WEDNESDAY	Due Date	Done
		☐
		☐
		☐
		☐
		☐
		☐

📘 WORD OF THE WEEK

THURSDAY	Due Date	Done
		☐
		☐
		☐
		☐
		☐
		☐

FRIDAY	Due Date	Done
		☐
		☐
		☐
		☐
		☐
		☐

SATURDAY	Due Date	Done
		☐
		☐
		☐
		☐
		☐
		☐

SUNDAY	Due Date	Done
		☐
		☐
		☐
		☐
		☐
		☐

MONTH:

NOTES	SUNDAY	MONDAY	TUESDAY
	☐	☐	☐
	☐	☐	☐
	☐	☐	☐
	☐	☐	☐
	☐	☐	☐

WEDNESDAY	THURSDAY	FRIDAY	SATURDAY
☐	☐	☐	☐
☐	☐	☐	☐
☐	☐	☐	☐
☐	☐	☐	☐
☐	☐	☐	☐

WEEKLY PLANNING CHECKLIST `WEEK OF`

This week's goals are: ....
....

MONDAY	Due Date	Done
		☐
		☐
		☐
		☐
		☐
		☐

TUESDAY	Due Date	Done
		☐
		☐
		☐
		☐
		☐
		☐

WEDNESDAY	Due Date	Done
		☐
		☐
		☐
		☐
		☐
		☐

📕 **WORD OF THE WEEK**

THURSDAY	Due Date	Done
		☐
		☐
		☐
		☐
		☐
		☐

FRIDAY	Due Date	Done
		☐
		☐
		☐
		☐
		☐
		☐

SATURDAY	Due Date	Done
		☐
		☐
		☐
		☐
		☐
		☐

SUNDAY	Due Date	Done
		☐
		☐
		☐
		☐
		☐
		☐

WEEKLY PLANNING CHECKLIST — WEEK OF

This week's goals are: ....
....

MONDAY	Due Date	Done
		☐
		☐
		☐
		☐
		☐
		☐

TUESDAY	Due Date	Done
		☐
		☐
		☐
		☐
		☐
		☐

WEDNESDAY	Due Date	Done
		☐
		☐
		☐
		☐
		☐
		☐

📖 **WORD OF THE WEEK**

THURSDAY	Due Date	Done
		☐
		☐
		☐
		☐
		☐
		☐

FRIDAY	Due Date	Done
		☐
		☐
		☐
		☐
		☐
		☐

SATURDAY	Due Date	Done
		☐
		☐
		☐
		☐
		☐
		☐

SUNDAY	Due Date	Done
		☐
		☐
		☐
		☐
		☐
		☐

WEEKLY PLANNING CHECKLIST — WEEK OF

This week's goals are: ....
....

MONDAY	Due Date	Done
		☐
		☐
		☐
		☐
		☐
		☐

TUESDAY	Due Date	Done
		☐
		☐
		☐
		☐
		☐
		☐

WEDNESDAY	Due Date	Done
		☐
		☐
		☐
		☐
		☐
		☐

📖 WORD OF THE WEEK

THURSDAY	Due Date	Done
		☐
		☐
		☐
		☐
		☐
		☐

FRIDAY	Due Date	Done
		☐
		☐
		☐
		☐
		☐
		☐

SATURDAY	Due Date	Done
		☐
		☐
		☐
		☐
		☐
		☐

SUNDAY	Due Date	Done
		☐
		☐
		☐
		☐
		☐
		☐

WEEKLY PLANNING CHECKLIST   WEEK OF

This week's goals are: ....
....

MONDAY	Due Date	Done
		☐
		☐
		☐
		☐
		☐
		☐

TUESDAY	Due Date	Done
		☐
		☐
		☐
		☐
		☐
		☐

WEDNESDAY	Due Date	Done
		☐
		☐
		☐
		☐
		☐
		☐

📖 **WORD OF THE WEEK**

THURSDAY	Due Date	Done
		☐
		☐
		☐
		☐
		☐
		☐

FRIDAY	Due Date	Done
		☐
		☐
		☐
		☐
		☐
		☐

SATURDAY	Due Date	Done
		☐
		☐
		☐
		☐
		☐
		☐

SUNDAY	Due Date	Done
		☐
		☐
		☐
		☐
		☐
		☐

WEEKLY PLANNING CHECKLIST   WEEK OF

This week's goals are:

MONDAY	Due Date	Done
		☐
		☐
		☐
		☐
		☐
		☐

TUESDAY	Due Date	Done
		☐
		☐
		☐
		☐
		☐
		☐

WEDNESDAY	Due Date	Done
		☐
		☐
		☐
		☐
		☐
		☐

📖 WORD OF THE WEEK

THURSDAY	Due Date	Done
		☐
		☐
		☐
		☐
		☐
		☐

FRIDAY	Due Date	Done
		☐
		☐
		☐
		☐
		☐
		☐

SATURDAY	Due Date	Done
		☐
		☐
		☐
		☐
		☐
		☐

SUNDAY	Due Date	Done
		☐
		☐
		☐
		☐
		☐
		☐

MONTH:

NOTES	SUNDAY	MONDAY	TUESDAY
	☐	☐	☐
	☐	☐	☐
	☐	☐	☐
	☐	☐	☐
	☐	☐	☐

WEDNESDAY	THURSDAY	FRIDAY	SATURDAY

WEEKLY PLANNING CHECKLIST `WEEK OF`

This week's goals are: ....
....

MONDAY	Due Date	Done
		☐
		☐
		☐
		☐
		☐
		☐

TUESDAY	Due Date	Done
		☐
		☐
		☐
		☐
		☐
		☐

WEDNESDAY	Due Date	Done
		☐
		☐
		☐
		☐
		☐
		☐

📖 **WORD OF THE WEEK**

PART II: FOCUS AND ORGANIZATION ARE KEYS FOR SUCCESS

THURSDAY	Due Date	Done
		☐
		☐
		☐
		☐
		☐
		☐

FRIDAY	Due Date	Done
		☐
		☐
		☐
		☐
		☐
		☐

SATURDAY	Due Date	Done
		☐
		☐
		☐
		☐
		☐
		☐

SUNDAY	Due Date	Done
		☐
		☐
		☐
		☐
		☐
		☐

WEEKLY PLANNING CHECKLIST **WEEK OF**

This week's goals are: ....
....

MONDAY	Due Date	Done
		☐
		☐
		☐
		☐
		☐
		☐

TUESDAY	Due Date	Done
		☐
		☐
		☐
		☐
		☐
		☐

WEDNESDAY	Due Date	Done
		☐
		☐
		☐
		☐
		☐
		☐

📖 **WORD OF THE WEEK**

THURSDAY	Due Date	Done
		☐
		☐
		☐
		☐
		☐
		☐

FRIDAY	Due Date	Done
		☐
		☐
		☐
		☐
		☐
		☐

SATURDAY	Due Date	Done
		☐
		☐
		☐
		☐
		☐
		☐

SUNDAY	Due Date	Done
		☐
		☐
		☐
		☐
		☐
		☐

WEEKLY PLANNING CHECKLIST — WEEK OF

This week's goals are: ....
....

MONDAY	Due Date	Done
		☐
		☐
		☐
		☐
		☐
		☐

TUESDAY	Due Date	Done
		☐
		☐
		☐
		☐
		☐
		☐

WEDNESDAY	Due Date	Done
		☐
		☐
		☐
		☐
		☐
		☐

📖 WORD OF THE WEEK

THURSDAY	Due Date	Done
		☐
		☐
		☐
		☐
		☐
		☐

FRIDAY	Due Date	Done
		☐
		☐
		☐
		☐
		☐
		☐

SATURDAY	Due Date	Done
		☐
		☐
		☐
		☐
		☐
		☐

SUNDAY	Due Date	Done
		☐
		☐
		☐
		☐
		☐
		☐

WEEKLY PLANNING CHECKLIST   WEEK OF

This week's goals are: ....
....

MONDAY	Due Date	Done
		☐
		☐
		☐
		☐
		☐
		☐

TUESDAY	Due Date	Done
		☐
		☐
		☐
		☐
		☐
		☐

WEDNESDAY	Due Date	Done
		☐
		☐
		☐
		☐
		☐
		☐

📖 **WORD OF THE WEEK**

THURSDAY	Due Date	Done
		☐
		☐
		☐
		☐
		☐
		☐

FRIDAY	Due Date	Done
		☐
		☐
		☐
		☐
		☐
		☐

SATURDAY	Due Date	Done
		☐
		☐
		☐
		☐
		☐
		☐

SUNDAY	Due Date	Done
		☐
		☐
		☐
		☐
		☐
		☐

WEEKLY PLANNING CHECKLIST WEEK OF

This week's goals are: ....
....

MONDAY	Due Date	Done
		☐
		☐
		☐
		☐
		☐
		☐

TUESDAY	Due Date	Done
		☐
		☐
		☐
		☐
		☐
		☐

WEDNESDAY	Due Date	Done
		☐
		☐
		☐
		☐
		☐
		☐

📖 **WORD OF THE WEEK**

THURSDAY	Due Date	Done
		☐
		☐
		☐
		☐
		☐
		☐

FRIDAY	Due Date	Done
		☐
		☐
		☐
		☐
		☐
		☐

SATURDAY	Due Date	Done
		☐
		☐
		☐
		☐
		☐
		☐

SUNDAY	Due Date	Done
		☐
		☐
		☐
		☐
		☐
		☐

MONTH:

NOTES	SUNDAY	MONDAY	TUESDAY
	☐	☐	☐
	☐	☐	☐
	☐	☐	☐
	☐	☐	☐
	☐	☐	☐

WEDNESDAY	THURSDAY	FRIDAY	SATURDAY

WEEKLY PLANNING CHECKLIST **WEEK OF**

This week's goals are: ....
....

MONDAY	Due Date	Done
		☐
		☐
		☐
		☐
		☐
		☐

TUESDAY	Due Date	Done
		☐
		☐
		☐
		☐
		☐
		☐

WEDNESDAY	Due Date	Done
		☐
		☐
		☐
		☐
		☐
		☐

📕 **WORD OF THE WEEK**

THURSDAY	Due Date	Done
		☐
		☐
		☐
		☐
		☐
		☐

FRIDAY	Due Date	Done
		☐
		☐
		☐
		☐
		☐
		☐

SATURDAY	Due Date	Done
		☐
		☐
		☐
		☐
		☐
		☐

SUNDAY	Due Date	Done
		☐
		☐
		☐
		☐
		☐
		☐

WEEKLY PLANNING CHECKLIST **WEEK OF**

This week's goals are: ....
....

MONDAY	Due Date	Done
		☐
		☐
		☐
		☐
		☐
		☐

TUESDAY	Due Date	Done
		☐
		☐
		☐
		☐
		☐
		☐

WEDNESDAY	Due Date	Done
		☐
		☐
		☐
		☐
		☐
		☐

📖 **WORD OF THE WEEK**

THURSDAY	Due Date	Done
		☐
		☐
		☐
		☐
		☐
		☐

FRIDAY	Due Date	Done
		☐
		☐
		☐
		☐
		☐
		☐

SATURDAY	Due Date	Done
		☐
		☐
		☐
		☐
		☐
		☐

SUNDAY	Due Date	Done
		☐
		☐
		☐
		☐
		☐
		☐

WEEKLY PLANNING CHECKLIST WEEK OF

This week's goals are: ....
....

MONDAY	Due Date	Done
		☐
		☐
		☐
		☐
		☐
		☐

TUESDAY	Due Date	Done
		☐
		☐
		☐
		☐
		☐
		☐

WEDNESDAY	Due Date	Done
		☐
		☐
		☐
		☐
		☐
		☐

📕 **WORD OF THE WEEK**

THURSDAY	Due Date	Done
		☐
		☐
		☐
		☐
		☐
		☐

FRIDAY	Due Date	Done
		☐
		☐
		☐
		☐
		☐
		☐

SATURDAY	Due Date	Done
		☐
		☐
		☐
		☐
		☐
		☐

SUNDAY	Due Date	Done
		☐
		☐
		☐
		☐
		☐
		☐

WEEKLY PLANNING CHECKLIST   WEEK OF

This week's goals are: ....
....

MONDAY	Due Date	Done
		☐
		☐
		☐
		☐
		☐
		☐

TUESDAY	Due Date	Done
		☐
		☐
		☐
		☐
		☐
		☐

WEDNESDAY	Due Date	Done
		☐
		☐
		☐
		☐
		☐
		☐

📖 **WORD OF THE WEEK**

THURSDAY	Due Date	Done
		☐
		☐
		☐
		☐
		☐
		☐

FRIDAY	Due Date	Done
		☐
		☐
		☐
		☐
		☐
		☐

SATURDAY	Due Date	Done
		☐
		☐
		☐
		☐
		☐
		☐

SUNDAY	Due Date	Done
		☐
		☐
		☐
		☐
		☐
		☐

WEEKLY PLANNING CHECKLIST — WEEK OF

This week's goals are: ....
....

MONDAY	Due Date	Done
		☐
		☐
		☐
		☐
		☐
		☐

TUESDAY	Due Date	Done
		☐
		☐
		☐
		☐
		☐
		☐

WEDNESDAY	Due Date	Done
		☐
		☐
		☐
		☐
		☐
		☐

📖 **WORD OF THE WEEK**

THURSDAY	Due Date	Done
		☐
		☐
		☐
		☐
		☐
		☐

FRIDAY	Due Date	Done
		☐
		☐
		☐
		☐
		☐
		☐

SATURDAY	Due Date	Done
		☐
		☐
		☐
		☐
		☐
		☐

SUNDAY	Due Date	Done
		☐
		☐
		☐
		☐
		☐
		☐

MONTH:

NOTES	SUNDAY	MONDAY	TUESDAY
	☐	☐	☐
	☐	☐	☐
	☐	☐	☐
	☐	☐	☐
	☐	☐	☐

WEDNESDAY	THURSDAY	FRIDAY	SATURDAY

WEEKLY PLANNING CHECKLIST   WEEK OF

This week's goals are: ....
....

MONDAY	Due Date	Done
		☐
		☐
		☐
		☐
		☐
		☐

TUESDAY	Due Date	Done
		☐
		☐
		☐
		☐
		☐
		☐

WEDNESDAY	Due Date	Done
		☐
		☐
		☐
		☐
		☐
		☐

📕 **WORD OF THE WEEK**

THURSDAY	Due Date	Done
		☐
		☐
		☐
		☐
		☐
		☐

FRIDAY	Due Date	Done
		☐
		☐
		☐
		☐
		☐
		☐

SATURDAY	Due Date	Done
		☐
		☐
		☐
		☐
		☐
		☐

SUNDAY	Due Date	Done
		☐
		☐
		☐
		☐
		☐
		☐

WEEKLY PLANNING CHECKLIST   WEEK OF

This week's goals are: ....
....

MONDAY	Due Date	Done
		☐
		☐
		☐
		☐
		☐
		☐

TUESDAY	Due Date	Done
		☐
		☐
		☐
		☐
		☐
		☐

WEDNESDAY	Due Date	Done
		☐
		☐
		☐
		☐
		☐
		☐

📘 **WORD OF THE WEEK**

THURSDAY	Due Date	Done
		☐
		☐
		☐
		☐
		☐
		☐

FRIDAY	Due Date	Done
		☐
		☐
		☐
		☐
		☐
		☐

SATURDAY	Due Date	Done
		☐
		☐
		☐
		☐
		☐
		☐

SUNDAY	Due Date	Done
		☐
		☐
		☐
		☐
		☐
		☐

WEEKLY PLANNING CHECKLIST — WEEK OF

This week's goals are: ....
....

MONDAY	Due Date	Done
		☐
		☐
		☐
		☐
		☐
		☐

TUESDAY	Due Date	Done
		☐
		☐
		☐
		☐
		☐
		☐

WEDNESDAY	Due Date	Done
		☐
		☐
		☐
		☐
		☐
		☐

📖 **WORD OF THE WEEK**

THURSDAY	Due Date	Done
		☐
		☐
		☐
		☐
		☐
		☐

FRIDAY	Due Date	Done
		☐
		☐
		☐
		☐
		☐
		☐

SATURDAY	Due Date	Done
		☐
		☐
		☐
		☐
		☐
		☐

SUNDAY	Due Date	Done
		☐
		☐
		☐
		☐
		☐
		☐

WEEKLY PLANNING CHECKLIST   WEEK OF

This week's goals are: ....
....

MONDAY	Due Date	Done
		☐
		☐
		☐
		☐
		☐
		☐

TUESDAY	Due Date	Done
		☐
		☐
		☐
		☐
		☐
		☐

WEDNESDAY	Due Date	Done
		☐
		☐
		☐
		☐
		☐
		☐

WORD OF THE WEEK

THURSDAY	Due Date	Done
		☐
		☐
		☐
		☐
		☐
		☐

FRIDAY	Due Date	Done
		☐
		☐
		☐
		☐
		☐
		☐

SATURDAY	Due Date	Done
		☐
		☐
		☐
		☐
		☐
		☐

SUNDAY	Due Date	Done
		☐
		☐
		☐
		☐
		☐
		☐

WEEKLY PLANNING CHECKLIST **WEEK OF**

This week's goals are: ....
....

MONDAY	Due Date	Done
		☐
		☐
		☐
		☐
		☐
		☐

TUESDAY	Due Date	Done
		☐
		☐
		☐
		☐
		☐
		☐

WEDNESDAY	Due Date	Done
		☐
		☐
		☐
		☐
		☐
		☐

WORD OF THE WEEK

THURSDAY	Due Date	Done
		☐
		☐
		☐
		☐
		☐
		☐

FRIDAY	Due Date	Done
		☐
		☐
		☐
		☐
		☐
		☐

SATURDAY	Due Date	Done
		☐
		☐
		☐
		☐
		☐
		☐

SUNDAY	Due Date	Done
		☐
		☐
		☐
		☐
		☐
		☐

★ Part III ★

Prioritize
BE DISCIPLINED AND PRODUCTIVE

INTRODUCTION TO PART III

Did you know you cannot buy time? Everyone in the world is given 24 hours to manage every day. How efficiently and effectively you manage the 24 hours you are given will determine your success. I am confident that most, if not all, successful people will argue that their ability to properly manage their time is central to their success.

WHAT IS TIME MANAGEMENT?

According to the *Cambridge Dictionary*, "Time management is the practice of using the time that you have available in a useful and effective way, especially in your work."

Time management requires discipline, and it is a fundamental principle in life. If you can master this principle, you will be successful.

THE WEEKLY TIME MANAGEMENT GRID

In any student's life, there is a myriad of things that must be done: attending classes and lectures, tending to chores at home, completing assignments, engaging in extracurricular activities, and sleeping. Everything requires time, and you must learn how to prioritize, be productive, disciplined, and adequately plan your days.

As a student, you may rely on your memory, jot down information using an electronic device of choice, or write out lists of tasks in various books. You simply have a to-do list; once a task is completed, you cross it out. This method lacks the proper structure and organization you need to succeed. Improper planning can lead to anxiety, poor grades, stress, fear, and frustration.

The Weekly Time Management Grid can help you eliminate these problems. It provides a visual representation of how you intend to spend your time on any given day and week. This grid is designed to help you focus, practice self-discipline, prioritize, organize, be productive, and reduce procrastination.

HOW TO USE IT

Start by blocking out what is consistent in your life, such as the time you spend at school or university, sleeping, and eating.

You can divide your time by using the time-blocking technique: blocking out specific times for certain activities. Alternatively, you can use arrows or brackets to assign a specified task or activity to a particular time. To make the exercise more fun, you may want to color-coordinate specific tasks or types of tasks. For example, you could use red to represent breaks or yellow to represent time spent sleeping.

Assign specific work, assignments, chores, or any task recorded on your Weekly Planning Checklist to the Weekly Time Management Grid.

If you wish to watch a movie, attend a social function, or do anything else that requires a significant amount of time, make sure to schedule the event and account for the specific amount of time you intend to use to engage in the activity.

It is essential to work on your Weekly Time Management Grid every week. If you find that you cannot complete a task in the time that has been allotted, do not get frustrated or overwhelmed. Remember, consistency is the key. The more you commit to this technique, the more efficiently you will be at discovering what works best for you.

MAKE PROPER USE OF YOUR TIME

Account for all your time, including your free time. What's free time? It can be the hour before classes begin, lunchtime, the time you spend in the car, the time you spend on the bus, or the time you spend walking to and from school.

You may use these times to review your classwork or listen to a recorded class or lecture. Alternatively, you may decide to study, meet with a teacher or lecturer, visit the library to do research, or use an electronic device to assist with research. Remember the adage, "Time wasted is gone forever." You will be more structured, more focused, and more intentional about your work when you adequately account for your time.

WHEN TO STUDY

Every student is different. Some students work better early in the morning, and others work better in the evening. You must figure out what is your best time to study.

BREAKS

It is crucial to take breaks when you are studying or completing homework assignments. A break should not last an hour. A break should last for 5–15 minutes after you have completed a task. The length of time to use for a break should be determined by the intensity of the task you have completed.

During your breaks, you can check your cell phone, stretch your legs or get a snack. Do not participate in anything that may become a prolonged distraction, such as watching a television program or playing a video game.

Appropriate breaks will allow your mind to rest and enable you to reset and refocus.

ALWAYS REMEMBER

When reviewing your classwork or lecture notes, the rule is that for every hour you spend in class or lecture, you should spend at least two hours reviewing the subject area. Always set aside time to review your classwork or lecture notes on the same day; this will aid in retention. Set priorities; spend more time on your more challenging classes and less time on those that are easy. When studying, the same rule applies—spend more time on your difficult subject areas and less time on the subject areas that are easier to manage. The key is to be determined, intentional, and responsible when managing your time on the Weekly Time Management Grid. Once you make this a habit, you will have more control over each day.

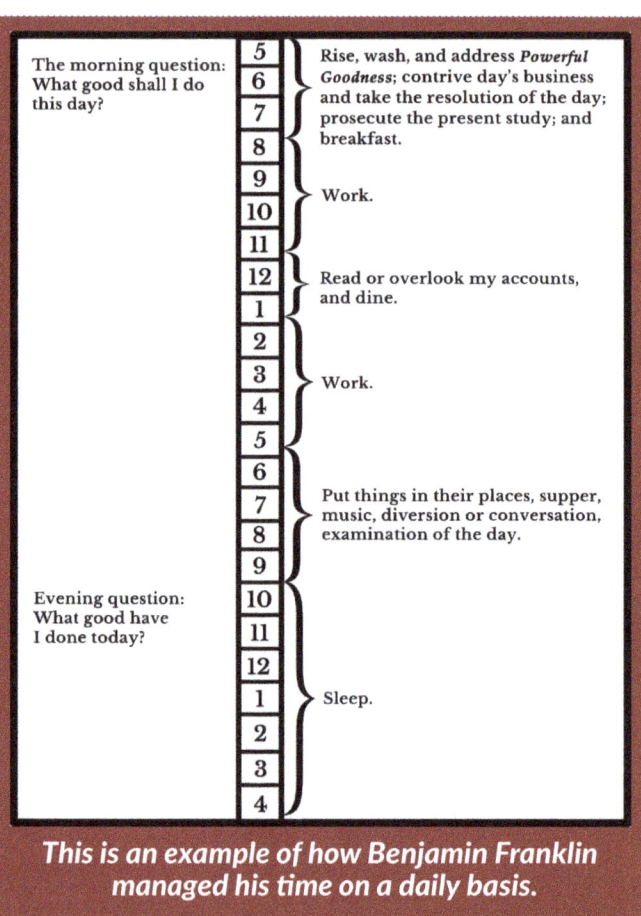

This is an example of how Benjamin Franklin managed his time on a daily basis.

Students, achieving success takes time, commitment, and determination. A to-do list is just that—things you must do, but a planner will help you focus on, organize, and execute your tasks. Many of the most influential people around the world, such as Bill Gates, Jack Dorsey, Elon Musk, and even as far back as Benjamin Franklin, have discovered the value of having a structured time management system. I encourage you to embrace this time-tested technique to maximize your potential.

WEEKLY AFFIRMATIONS

You are encouraged to affirm yourself with a positive statement every week, regularly repeat it, and believe it. Stay positive along your journey on the road to success. Be motivated as you embrace your goals. You can do it!

PART III: PRIORITIZE – BE DISCIPLINED AND PRODUCTIVE

WEEKLY TIME MANAGEMENT GRID

WEEK OF ....

This week's affirmation: ....

🕐	MONDAY	TUESDAY	WEDNESDAY	THURSDAY	FRIDAY	SATURDAY	SUNDAY

"Despair gives courage to a coward." ★ **Anonymous**

WEEKLY TIME MANAGEMENT GRID

WEEK OF ....

This week's affirmation: ....

🕐	MONDAY	TUESDAY	WEDNESDAY	THURSDAY	FRIDAY	SATURDAY	SUNDAY

"Only he who keeps his eye fixed on the far horizon will find his right road."

★ Dag Hammarskjold

WEEKLY TIME MANAGEMENT GRID

WEEK OF ....

This week's affirmation: ....

⏲	MONDAY	TUESDAY	WEDNESDAY	THURSDAY	FRIDAY	SATURDAY	SUNDAY

"The immature mind hops from one thing to another; the mature mind seeks to follow through."

★ **Harry A. Overstreet**

WEEKLY TIME MANAGEMENT GRID

WEEK OF ....

This week's affirmation: ....

🕐	MONDAY	TUESDAY	WEDNESDAY	THURSDAY	FRIDAY	SATURDAY	SUNDAY

"The secret to success in any human endeavor is total concentration." ★ **Kurt Vonnegut**

WEEKLY TIME MANAGEMENT GRID

WEEK OF ....

This week's affirmation: ....

⏱	MONDAY	TUESDAY	WEDNESDAY	THURSDAY	FRIDAY	SATURDAY	SUNDAY

"The ability to concentrate and to use your time well is everything." ★ Lee Iacocca

WEEKLY TIME MANAGEMENT GRID

WEEK OF ....

This week's affirmation: ....

	MONDAY	TUESDAY	WEDNESDAY	THURSDAY	FRIDAY	SATURDAY	SUNDAY

"Do whatever you do intensely." ★ Robert Henri

PART III: PRIORITIZE – BE DISCIPLINED AND PRODUCTIVE

WEEKLY TIME MANAGEMENT GRID

WEEK OF ....

This week's affirmation: ....

⏲	MONDAY	TUESDAY	WEDNESDAY	THURSDAY	FRIDAY	SATURDAY	SUNDAY

"Having a dream isn't stupid. It's not having a dream that's stupid." ★ Anonymous

WEEKLY TIME MANAGEMENT GRID

WEEK OF ....

This week's affirmation: ....

🕐	MONDAY	TUESDAY	WEDNESDAY	THURSDAY	FRIDAY	SATURDAY	SUNDAY

"If you don't know where you are going, how can you expect to get there?" ★ **Basil S. Walsh**

PART III: PRIORITIZE – BE DISCIPLINED AND PRODUCTIVE

WEEKLY TIME MANAGEMENT GRID

WEEK OF

This week's affirmation:

	MONDAY	TUESDAY	WEDNESDAY	THURSDAY	FRIDAY	SATURDAY	SUNDAY

"The secret of success is constancy to purpose." ★ Benjamin Franklin

WEEKLY TIME MANAGEMENT GRID

WEEK OF ....

This week's affirmation: ....

🕐	MONDAY	TUESDAY	WEDNESDAY	THURSDAY	FRIDAY	SATURDAY	SUNDAY

"The tragedy of life doesn't lie in not reaching your goal. The tragedy lies in having no goal to reach." ★ **Benjamin Mays**

PART III: PRIORITIZE – BE DISCIPLINED AND PRODUCTIVE

WEEKLY TIME MANAGEMENT GRID

WEEK OF ....

This week's affirmation: ....

🕐	MONDAY	TUESDAY	WEDNESDAY	THURSDAY	FRIDAY	SATURDAY	SUNDAY

"Get out of the blocks, run your race, stay relaxed. If you run your race, you'll win. Channel your energy. Focus." ★ Carol Lewis

WEEKLY TIME MANAGEMENT GRID

WEEK OF ....

This week's affirmation: ....

⏱	MONDAY	TUESDAY	WEDNESDAY	THURSDAY	FRIDAY	SATURDAY	SUNDAY

"Purpose is what gives life a meaning." ★ C. H. Parkhurst

PART III: PRIORITIZE – BE DISCIPLINED AND PRODUCTIVE

WEEKLY TIME MANAGEMENT GRID

WEEK OF ....

This week's affirmation: ....

	MONDAY	TUESDAY	WEDNESDAY	THURSDAY	FRIDAY	SATURDAY	SUNDAY

"You have to have a dream so you can get up in the morning." ★ Billy Wilder

WEEKLY TIME MANAGEMENT GRID

WEEK OF ....

This week's affirmation: ....

⏰	MONDAY	TUESDAY	WEDNESDAY	THURSDAY	FRIDAY	SATURDAY	SUNDAY

"You must have long-range goals to keep you from being frustrated by short-range failures."

★ Charles C. Noble

PART III: PRIORITIZE – BE DISCIPLINED AND PRODUCTIVE

WEEKLY TIME MANAGEMENT GRID

WEEK OF ....

This week's affirmation: ....

⏱	MONDAY	TUESDAY	WEDNESDAY	THURSDAY	FRIDAY	SATURDAY	SUNDAY

"Everything's in the mind. That's where it all starts. Knowing what you want is the first step toward getting it." ★ Mae West

WEEKLY TIME MANAGEMENT GRID

WEEK OF ....

This week's affirmation: ....
....

🕐	MONDAY	TUESDAY	WEDNESDAY	THURSDAY	FRIDAY	SATURDAY	SUNDAY

"Concentrate on finding your goal then concentrate on reaching it." ★ **Colonel Michael Friedman**

WEEKLY TIME MANAGEMENT GRID

WEEK OF

This week's affirmation:

⏱	MONDAY	TUESDAY	WEDNESDAY	THURSDAY	FRIDAY	SATURDAY	SUNDAY

"Goals are dreams with deadlines." ★ Diana Scharf Hunt

WEEKLY TIME MANAGEMENT GRID

WEEK OF ....

This week's affirmation: ....
....

🕐	MONDAY	TUESDAY	WEDNESDAY	THURSDAY	FRIDAY	SATURDAY	SUNDAY

"He who demands little gets it." ★ Ellen Glasgow

WEEKLY TIME MANAGEMENT GRID

WEEK OF ....

This week's affirmation: ....

🕐	MONDAY	TUESDAY	WEDNESDAY	THURSDAY	FRIDAY	SATURDAY	SUNDAY

"First say to yourself what you would be, and then do what you have to do." ★ Epictetus

WEEKLY TIME MANAGEMENT GRID

WEEK OF ....

This week's affirmation: ....

🕐	MONDAY	TUESDAY	WEDNESDAY	THURSDAY	FRIDAY	SATURDAY	SUNDAY

"Remember if people talk behind your back, it only means you're two steps ahead!"

★ **Fannie Flagg**

WEEKLY TIME MANAGEMENT GRID

WEEK OF ....

This week's affirmation: ....

🕐	MONDAY	TUESDAY	WEDNESDAY	THURSDAY	FRIDAY	SATURDAY	SUNDAY

"People don't pay much attention to you when you are second best. I wanted to see what it felt like to be number one." ★ **Florence Griffith Joyner**

WEEKLY TIME MANAGEMENT GRID

WEEK OF ....

This week's affirmation: ....

🕐	MONDAY	TUESDAY	WEDNESDAY	THURSDAY	FRIDAY	SATURDAY	SUNDAY

"Man can only receive what he sees himself receiving." ★ **Florence Scovel Shinn**

PART III: PRIORITIZE – BE DISCIPLINED AND PRODUCTIVE

WEEKLY TIME MANAGEMENT GRID

WEEK OF

This week's affirmation:

	MONDAY	TUESDAY	WEDNESDAY	THURSDAY	FRIDAY	SATURDAY	SUNDAY

"Only he who can see the invisible can do the impossible." ★ Frank Gaines

WEEKLY TIME MANAGEMENT GRID

WEEK OF ....

This week's affirmation: ....

⏰	MONDAY	TUESDAY	WEDNESDAY	THURSDAY	FRIDAY	SATURDAY	SUNDAY

"Happiness lies in the joy of achievement and the thrill of creative effort."

★ **Franklin Delano Roosevelt**

WEEKLY TIME MANAGEMENT GRID

WEEK OF ....

This week's affirmation: ....

🕐	MONDAY	TUESDAY	WEDNESDAY	THURSDAY	FRIDAY	SATURDAY	SUNDAY

"In this life we get only those things for which we hunt, for which we strive, and for which we are willing to sacrifice." ★ George Matthew Adams

WEEKLY TIME MANAGEMENT GRID

WEEK OF ....

This week's affirmation: ....

🕐	MONDAY	TUESDAY	WEDNESDAY	THURSDAY	FRIDAY	SATURDAY	SUNDAY

"Obstacles are those frightful things you see when you take your eyes off the goal."

★ **Hannah More**

PART III: PRIORITIZE – BE DISCIPLINED AND PRODUCTIVE

WEEKLY TIME MANAGEMENT GRID

WEEK OF

This week's affirmation:

	MONDAY	TUESDAY	WEDNESDAY	THURSDAY	FRIDAY	SATURDAY	SUNDAY

"The poor man is not he who is without a cent, but he who is without a dream."

★ Harry Kemp

WEEKLY TIME MANAGEMENT GRID

WEEK OF ....

This week's affirmation: ....

⏰	MONDAY	TUESDAY	WEDNESDAY	THURSDAY	FRIDAY	SATURDAY	SUNDAY

"Once you say you're going to settle for second, that's what happens to you."

★ John F. Kennedy

WEEKLY TIME MANAGEMENT GRID

WEEK OF ....

This week's affirmation: ....

⏱	MONDAY	TUESDAY	WEDNESDAY	THURSDAY	FRIDAY	SATURDAY	SUNDAY

"The very first condition of lasting happiness is that a life should be full of purpose, aiming at something outside self." ★ Hugh Black

WEEKLY TIME MANAGEMENT GRID

WEEK OF ....

This week's affirmation: ....
....

	MONDAY	TUESDAY	WEDNESDAY	THURSDAY	FRIDAY	SATURDAY	SUNDAY

"Why should I deem myself to be a chisel, when I could be the artist?"

★ J. C. F. von Schiller

WEEKLY TIME MANAGEMENT GRID

WEEK OF ....

This week's affirmation: ....

	MONDAY	TUESDAY	WEDNESDAY	THURSDAY	FRIDAY	SATURDAY	SUNDAY

"Aim at the sun, and you may not reach it; but your arrow will fly far higher than if aimed at an object on a level with yourself." ★ J. Hawes

WEEKLY TIME MANAGEMENT GRID

WEEK OF

This week's affirmation:

🕐	MONDAY	TUESDAY	WEDNESDAY	THURSDAY	FRIDAY	SATURDAY	SUNDAY

"An aim in life is the only fortune worth finding." ★ Jacqueline Kennedy Onassis

PART III: PRIORITIZE – BE DISCIPLINED AND PRODUCTIVE

WEEKLY TIME MANAGEMENT GRID

WEEK OF

This week's affirmation:

	MONDAY	TUESDAY	WEDNESDAY	THURSDAY	FRIDAY	SATURDAY	SUNDAY

"A useless life is an early death." ★ Johann von Goethe

WEEKLY TIME MANAGEMENT GRID

WEEK OF ....

This week's affirmation: ....

🕐	MONDAY	TUESDAY	WEDNESDAY	THURSDAY	FRIDAY	SATURDAY	SUNDAY

"Happiness is not the end of life; character is." ★ Henry Ward Beecher

PART III: PRIORITIZE – BE DISCIPLINED AND PRODUCTIVE

WEEKLY TIME MANAGEMENT GRID

WEEK OF

This week's affirmation:

	MONDAY	TUESDAY	WEDNESDAY	THURSDAY	FRIDAY	SATURDAY	SUNDAY

"A person can grow only as much as his horizon allows." ★ John Powell

WEEKLY TIME MANAGEMENT GRID

WEEK OF ....

This week's affirmation: ....

🕐	MONDAY	TUESDAY	WEDNESDAY	THURSDAY	FRIDAY	SATURDAY	SUNDAY

"Before you begin a thing, remind yourself that difficulties and delays quite impossible to foresee are ahead. You can only see one thing clearly and that is your goal. Form a mental vision of that and cling to it through thick and thin." ★ **Kathleen Norris**

WEEKLY TIME MANAGEMENT GRID

WEEK OF ....

This week's affirmation: ....

🕐	MONDAY	TUESDAY	WEDNESDAY	THURSDAY	FRIDAY	SATURDAY	SUNDAY

"I think the purpose of life is to be useful, to be responsible, to be honorable, to be compassionate. It is, after all, to matter: to count, to stand for something, to have made some difference that you lived at all." ★ **Leo C. Rosten**

WEEKLY TIME MANAGEMENT GRID

WEEK OF ....

This week's affirmation: ....

⏰	MONDAY	TUESDAY	WEDNESDAY	THURSDAY	FRIDAY	SATURDAY	SUNDAY

"A good goal is like a strenuous exercise—it makes you stretch." ★ Mary Kay Ash

PART III: PRIORITIZE – BE DISCIPLINED AND PRODUCTIVE

WEEKLY TIME MANAGEMENT GRID

WEEK OF

This week's affirmation:

🕐	MONDAY	TUESDAY	WEDNESDAY	THURSDAY	FRIDAY	SATURDAY	SUNDAY

"I always ask the question, 'Is this what I want in my life?'" ★ Kathy Ireland

WEEKLY TIME MANAGEMENT GRID

WEEK OF ....

This week's affirmation: ....

🕐	MONDAY	TUESDAY	WEDNESDAY	THURSDAY	FRIDAY	SATURDAY	SUNDAY

"Aim at perfection in everything, though in most things it is unattainable. However, they who aim at it, and persevere, will come much nearer to it than those whose laziness and despondency make them give it up as unattainable." ★ **Lord Chesterfield**

WEEKLY TIME MANAGEMENT GRID

WEEK OF ....

This week's affirmation: ....

🕐	MONDAY	TUESDAY	WEDNESDAY	THURSDAY	FRIDAY	SATURDAY	SUNDAY

"I can tell you how to get what you want. You've just got to keep a thing in view and go for it and never let your eyes wander to right or left or up or down. And looking back is fatal." ★ William J. Lock

WEEKLY TIME MANAGEMENT GRID

WEEK OF ....

This week's affirmation: ....

	MONDAY	TUESDAY	WEDNESDAY	THURSDAY	FRIDAY	SATURDAY	SUNDAY

"You can change your beliefs so they empower your dreams and desires. Create a strong belief in yourself and what you want." ★ Marcia Wieder

PART III: PRIORITIZE – BE DISCIPLINED AND PRODUCTIVE

WEEKLY TIME MANAGEMENT GRID

WEEK OF ....

This week's affirmation: ....

🕐	MONDAY	TUESDAY	WEDNESDAY	THURSDAY	FRIDAY	SATURDAY	SUNDAY

"People think that at the top there isn't much room. They tend to think of it as an Everest. My message is that there is tons of room at the top." ★ Margaret Thatcher

WEEKLY TIME MANAGEMENT GRID

WEEK OF ....

This week's affirmation: ....

⏱	MONDAY	TUESDAY	WEDNESDAY	THURSDAY	FRIDAY	SATURDAY	SUNDAY

"If you just set out to be liked, you would be prepared to compromise on anything at any time, and you would achieve nothing." ★ Margaret Thatcher

PART III: PRIORITIZE – BE DISCIPLINED AND PRODUCTIVE

WEEKLY TIME MANAGEMENT GRID

WEEK OF ....

This week's affirmation: ....

	MONDAY	TUESDAY	WEDNESDAY	THURSDAY	FRIDAY	SATURDAY	SUNDAY

"When you reach for the stars, you may not quite get one, but you won't come up with a handful of mud, either." ★ Leo Burnett

WEEKLY TIME MANAGEMENT GRID

WEEK OF ....

This week's affirmation: ....

🕐	MONDAY	TUESDAY	WEDNESDAY	THURSDAY	FRIDAY	SATURDAY	SUNDAY

"You decide what it is you want to accomplish and then you lay out your plans to get there and then you just do it. It's pretty straightforward." ★ Nancy Ditz

WEEKLY TIME MANAGEMENT GRID

WEEK OF ....

This week's affirmation: ....

⏰	MONDAY	TUESDAY	WEDNESDAY	THURSDAY	FRIDAY	SATURDAY	SUNDAY

"Where no plan is laid, where the disposal of time is surrendered merely to the chance of incident, chaos will soon reign." ★ Victor Hugo

WEEKLY TIME MANAGEMENT GRID

WEEK OF ....

This week's affirmation: ....

🕐	MONDAY	TUESDAY	WEDNESDAY	THURSDAY	FRIDAY	SATURDAY	SUNDAY

"Never try to catch two frogs with one hand." ★ **Chinese proverb**

PART III: PRIORITIZE – BE DISCIPLINED AND PRODUCTIVE

WEEKLY TIME MANAGEMENT GRID

WEEK OF ....

This week's affirmation: ....

🕐	MONDAY	TUESDAY	WEDNESDAY	THURSDAY	FRIDAY	SATURDAY	SUNDAY

"The real essence of work is concentrated energy." ★ **Walter Bagehot**

WEEKLY TIME MANAGEMENT GRID

WEEK OF ....

This week's affirmation: ....
....

🕐	MONDAY	TUESDAY	WEDNESDAY	THURSDAY	FRIDAY	SATURDAY	SUNDAY

"Life is the sum of all your choices." ★ Albert Camus

★ Part IV ★

I Made It!

Reflections on the Past School Year

Personal Reading List

1. _____
2. _____
3. _____
4. _____
5. _____
6. _____
7. _____

"When all else is lost, the future still remains." ★ **Christian Nestell Bovee**

Forecast FOR THE NEXT SCHOOL YEAR

JULY _____

_____

_____

_____

AUGUST _____

_____

_____

_____

SEPTEMBER _____

_____

_____

_____

OCTOBER _____

_____

_____

_____

NOVEMBER _____

_____

_____

_____

DECEMBER _____

_____

_____

_____

JANUARY _____	APRIL _____
_____	_____
_____	_____
_____	_____

FEBRUARY _____	MAY _____
_____	_____
_____	_____
_____	_____

MARCH _____	JUNE _____
_____	_____
_____	_____
_____	_____

"I know of no way of judging the future but by the past." ★ Patrick Henry

ABOUT THE AUTHOR

Koschina L. Marshall is an attorney-at-law, a former educator in the public school system in the Commonwealth of The Bahamas, a former lecturer, faculty of law, the University of the West Indies/College of The Bahamas, and a former acting magistrate in the Juvenile Court in the Commonwealth of The Bahamas.

Koschina knows, first-hand, many of the challenges that students face on their journey to achieve academic success. She faced many challenges in her academic pursuit but was encouraged and coached along the way by family members and mentors who instilled lifelong principles that helped her to maximize her potential. Now she wants to share some of her time-tested principles with you.

Ms. Marshall firmly believes that students can maximize their full potential if they strive to become intentional, focus, practice self-discipline, prioritize, organize, be productive, and reduce procrastination. Her education series of successful tools to obtain academic success is coming soon.

Koschina can be reached at transformationalacademiccoach@gmail.com.

BIBLIOGRAPHY

Franklin, Benjamin, John Woolman, and William Penn. *The Autobiography of Benjamin Franklin; The Journal of John Woolman; Fruits of Solitude*. P.F. Collier, 1909.

Kelly, Joanne. *The Gigantic Book of Famous Quotations*. London, UK: Independently published, 2019.

Vale, David, Stephen Mullaney, and Leo Hartas. *The Cambridge Dictionary*. Cambridge: Cambridge University Press, 1996. "time management", accessed, October 17, 2021.

www.ingramcontent.com/pod-product-compliance
Lightning Source LLC
Chambersburg PA
CBHW041238240426
43661CB00070B/2917